Responding to children in the

Claire Cameron

IOE Press

Responding to children in the twenty-first century
Education, social pedagogy and belonging

Claire Cameron

Based on an Inaugural Professorial Lecture delivered at the UCL Institute of Education
on 20 February 2018

UCL Institute of Education Press
Professorial Lecture Series

Institute of Education

First published in 2018 by the UCL Institute of Education Press,
20 Bedford Way, London WC1H 0AL

www.ucl-ioe-press.com

British Library Cataloguing-in-Publication Data:
A catalogue record for this publication is available from the British Library

ISBNs
978-1-78277-241-5 (Paperback)
978-1-78277-242-2 (PDF eBook)
978-1-78277-243-9 (ePub eBook)
978-1-78277-244-6 (Kindle eBook)

Typeset by Quadrant Infotech (India) Pvt Ltd
Printed by ImageData Ltd

Biography

Claire Cameron is Professor of Social Pedagogy at the UCL Institute of Education, where since the early 1990s she has been researching issues of care, social pedagogy, gender, the children's workforce, looked-after children, and early childhood education and care. She is also Deputy Director of the Thomas Coram Research Unit (TCRU), a specialist social science research unit at the IOE.

Previously a social worker, she has conducted many studies, many cross-national, funded by government, the European Union and NGOs. She led the first European study of the higher education pathways of young people from public care backgrounds (also known as YiPPEE, 2008–11).

Responding to children in the twenty-first century

I have three children, now grown up. One day, driving to a music lesson, we were talking about my work as a social researcher. Talulla asked, pointedly, 'What have you found out, precisely?' In this lecture, I shall attempt to bring together some of that 'finding out', although anyone in the social sciences knows how provisional knowledge is.

Introduction

Now more than ever, children, young people and families are facing an unequal UK, but one in which the social and public visibility of children and childhood has never been greater. There are immense opportunities for young people to participate in the social and political world. The legitimacy of 'children's voices' in public discourse is now established. But, at the same time, child poverty is again rising (Joseph Rowntree Foundation, 2017), the number of children in care is increasing (DfE, 2017) and services to support children, young people and families through care and education are being deeply damaged through austerity measures (Butler, 2017; Hastings *et al.*, 2015). In addition, the trajectories of young people – particularly those without supportive and materially resourceful families – are being, and have been for some time, deliberately targeted, so as to shape their options quite narrowly (Schoon and Lyons-Amos, 2017). With demand rising, resources shrinking and polarization rather than consensus-building as the dominant political mantra, the metaphors of 'cliff edge', 'pressure cooker' and 'launch into the unknown' seem very apt for today's generation of children and young people.

In this lecture I am going to argue that the way in which we, as societies, adults, parents, policymakers, practitioners, leaders and academics choose to respond to children and young people in terms of the values held, the concepts that frame thinking, and action, and what we actually do, can make a clear difference to the quality of life for children and young people. There may well be a cyclical dimension, in that the way we practise (in the broadest sense) may have implications for how our children's generation practises towards us as older and more dependent people. But that is beyond the scope of today's talk. Clearly, there are also major structural forces at work that shape social and educational practice, but beyond the context setting above, discussion of these is mostly outside my scope.

I am going to try to draw a 'red thread' through my research and development work, which has mostly taken place at Thomas Coram Research Unit (TCRU), Institute of Education, now a faculty of University College London. Research and biography are often linked and I am no exception. I am going to start in a biographical way, by introducing you to a very formative educational experience at a small progressive educational school in Scotland, called Kilquhanity House. I was able to draw on this experience when I began researching social pedagogy as part of a series of studies conducted at TCRU. These studies examined the potential of different, Continental European, approaches to practices addressing the very poor quality of life and outcomes for children living in foster care or residential care. The relationship between education and social pedagogy as a framework for professional practice is one major theme of my research. A second theme is the children's workforce. The relationship between the characteristics of the workforce, their professional education and operational context and what they actually do to shape children's lives was a key theme of several studies. Two studies I am going to draw on here are *Care Work in Europe: Current understandings and future directions*[1] and *Residential Care in Denmark, Germany and England.*[2]

A third theme is the experience of young people who have been in local authority care in terms of their education and how professional practice shapes their experience. *Young People from a Public Care Background: Pathways to education in Europe* (YiPPEE[3]) was a cross-national, multi-method examination of post-compulsory educational pathways in five European countries. It led to a knowledge-exchange programme around how schools can support the

---

1   Funded by the EU FP5 2001–4.
2   Funded by the Department of Health.
3   Funded by EU FP7 2008–11.

education of children in care at younger ages (Carroll and Cameron, 2017), and to further studies examining the longer-term trajectories for care leavers in terms of employment, health and family life (Cameron, 2016; Cameron *et al.*, 2018; Cameron *et al.*, submitted).

Finally, I am going to introduce some more recent work that promises to shape professional responses to children in care. This work focuses on a multidimensional concept of belonging as a social pedagogic response, as a way to reorient the conceptual base away from solely thinking about children's attachment to carers and towards being fully part of families and societies.

The children and young people I am thinking about in this lecture are mostly those who do not live with their birth families, largely due to abuse and neglect, family dysfunction or abandonment. My position is that the people in this group are children first and should not be defined solely by their adversity – as victims, dangerous or vulnerable – but should instead be treated as being as 'rich' as other children in terms of their talents and possibilities and with equal rights to education, a cultural life, health, friendships and love. Children in care should be, in the words of one of our interviewees, 'getting some possibilities in life'. Hence I want to start with *education* and its broader meaning.

What do I mean by 'education'?

Kilquhanity House, in the Galloway Hills, was modelled on A.S. Neill's Summerhill School in Suffolk, where lessons were optional and teachers were called by their first names. This was a 'free' school. Our headmaster at Kilquhanity, John Aitkenhead, said that education was about participation, creativity and the practical activities of living together. Looking back over 50 years of leading the school, in *Kilquhanity's Jubilee* (Cameron, 1990), John said:

> 'Education is the generation of happiness' (inspired by Herbert Read). It is not the pursuit of happiness; it is the involvement in activities and relationships, the creative work that nourishes the human spirit. (The word education is from the Latin word *educere*, to nourish.) Real, demanding situations abounded throughout these years. Kids frequently found themselves faced with the planning and building of the school. All the arts and crafts and skills involved made for real learning situations. The school farm was real. Adults and kids

shared all kinds of work on a basis of equality. The weekly meeting was real, dealing with actual living situations. All this was conducted in an atmosphere of freedom and underpinned by the principle of freedom, so that *learning proceeded in relaxed situations – an essential for success.* (emphasis added)

John Aitkenhead with a calf on the Kilquhanity House Farm.

Photo: *Scottish Field*

He went on:

Academic skills found their real level, their true worth, and we worked together and learned to live together, young and old, male and female, schooled and unschooled, skilled and unskilled. It was like a village, or, rather, an extended family or clan. Only there always seemed to be a specially high input of positive, happy, creative energy, the hallmark, in my opinion, of youngsters who are trusted, particularly when, for lack of money, and the usual hardware of schools, improvisation is the name of the game.

John (I cannot bring myself to refer to him by the more impersonal 'Aitkenhead' as he was always John to pupils and staff alike) wrote of his first visit to much more famous and more liberal Summerhill, in 1938:

... here were boys and girls of all ages and several colours and nations, living together and learning freedom, helping to make the rules of their small community. It was a new world in the context of schools, and to me it was intoxication.

This is clearly education in a broad sense. Attending lessons was only one part of the more general upbringing on offer, where participating in weekly council meetings was an important part of learning about self-government, and where being on first-name terms with teachers was a signifier of living in a community and of the importance of pastoral relationships to support learning. Also important were taking part in chores, in rotas or paid jobs, to keep the community life going.

The football pitch at Kilquhanity House.

Photo: unknown

Kilquhanity House council meeting, voting in action.

Photo: *Scottish Field*

Trying out a school-made go-kart.

Photo: Willie Galt

The school workshop.

Photo: Cassandra James

The school pony.

Photo: Cassandra James

The school cook.

Photo: Cassandra James

Education is clearly not like this in most of twenty-first-century Britain, although some examples exist of things being done differently. The 17 United World Colleges, which operate across four continents (Atlantic College in Wales is one) and bring together young people aged 16–19 to live and learn under the banner of 'education as a force to unite people, nations and cultures for peace and a sustainable future', come close. Or there's the Woodcraft Folk, a cooperatively run educational and empowerment organization in which groups of children and adults meet regularly and camp together periodically, with the shared values of peace, cooperation and equality. Another example is the Red Balloon Learner Group for bullied children, which works from the premise that attention to individual well-being and self-esteem is a highly important foundation for learning, and states: 'We provide an academic and therapeutic programme to enable our students to get back on track and reconnect with society.' Michael Fielding's work to recognize the important contribution of Alex Bloom to state education in England reminds us that in Bloom's secondary modern school in Stepney, London, in the 1950s, concepts of 'personalized learning', 'negotiated curriculum' and 'student voice' paved the way for more recent exercises in democratic education (Fielding, 2005). Bloom's approach had much in common with the practices at Kilquhanity House, with 'accustomed dialogue between teachers and students and a cumulative acceptance of a shared responsibility' for the well-being and progress of the school community (ibid.: 120).

But, in large part, *education* in England has become synonymous with the institution of *school*, with tests and attainment of exam passes, and performance in league tables. 'Behaviour' is no longer a neutral, descriptive, term but has become a reference to undesirable, problematic or simply bad behaviour. While children in England's schools are tested more than in any other European country (Eurydice, 2009), the demands of twenty-first-century employers are for more highly developed 'soft skills' and values such as communication, collaboration, a global mindset, navigation of networks and systems, and thinking creatively (CBI/Pearson, 2016).

While Kilquhanity House (in the 1970s) was far removed from this world, the values and skills it promoted, the elements of education that John talks about – practical doing, exercising commitment, working together, well-being or happiness in one's environment, democracy, self-government, freedom to choose (exercising self-regulation or knowing one's own mind) – have much in common with those now being identified as required for navigating the twenty-first century.

Education then, following Dewey and Kilquhanity, might be considered as being informed, respectful and wise. It has a collective dimension as well as an individual one. Education is:

- Deliberate and hopeful. It is learning we set out to make happen in the belief that people can 'be more'.
- Informed, respectful and wise. A process of inviting truth and possibility.
- Grounded in a desire that all may flourish and share in life. It is a cooperative and inclusive activity that looks to help people to live their lives as well as they can. (Smith, 2015)

Over some years at TCRU, and being part of the Institute of Education, we have troubled away at the different perspectives on 'education' in relation to early childhood services and in relation to education for looked-after children. In both cases, a divide between 'care' on the one hand and 'education' on the other, in terms of administrative responsibility, professionalization and concepts that guide actual practice, has been particularly unhelpful. We have come up with a two-dimensional phrasing:

- Education in a narrow sense – which refers to foregrounding the pursuit of academic achievement, over and above well-being, and being concerned with an agenda of prescribed curricula (rather than allowing knowledge to emerge), of tests, performance and league tables that invite competition and potentially exclusion of those who do not do well.
- Education in a broad sense – which refers to valuing both learning and the contexts in which children learn, valuing the diverse personhood of each individual, and the relational dimensions of learning. There is a holistic conception of the child as multidimensional.

By 'holistic' we are referring to an 'approach to work with people in which learning, care, health, general well-being and overall development are viewed as totally inseparable' (Boddy *et al.*, 2005). When working with children, holistic practice addresses the whole child, with his or her multiple dimensions, body, mind, creativity, history and social identity (Moss and Petrie, 2002).

In my book with Graham Connelly and Sonia Jackson, *Educating Children and Young People in Care: Learning placements and caring schools* (2015), we argued that education in a broad sense is about:

enabling children to grow up as citizens of a country equipped to take advantage of opportunities and realise ambitions, which may be both individual and social. By encouraging young people to adopt certain socially defined values and skills, education has a role in social cohesion, economic prosperity and in upholding democracy.

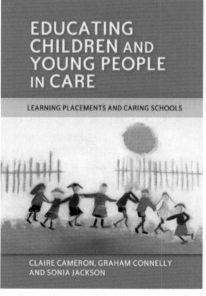

It's important to state that this is not an attempt to remove all assessed learning. Having externally validated learning is a very important part of its recognition. Rather, it's a restating of classical principles of education, or *educere* (as John Aitkenhead noted), meaning to draw out potential, and recognition of the relational dimensions of that drawing out in a democratic social world.

Reproduced by kind permission of Jessica Kingsley Publishers

In this concept of education, we respond to children as whole, multidimensional beings, we act with them and not on them and, alongside this relational approach, we are rooted in ideas of respect for both individuality and difference.

What do I mean by 'social pedagogy'?

Social pedagogy is a professional practice discipline that originated in nineteenth-century Germany and is found in many countries of the world that are influenced by Continental European thinking. It refers to practice that spans care and education, can be organized on an individual or collective basis, and is concerned with all-round development and upbringing for life in contemporary societies. It is very close to, or is, 'education in its broadest sense'. Another way of looking at social pedagogy is as 'bringing an educational lens to social problems'.

In the UK, social pedagogy is often valued for its attention to *professional-client/child relationships* in what is often regarded as the arena of direct practice social work – residential care, foster care, family support and so on. It is also a way of thinking about group settings such as youth work and work with care leavers; from an early childhood education perspective, in Denmark, the pedagogue is the major occupation working with young children in kindergartens and in out-of-school services. There is a clear *social justice* dimension to social pedagogy – it was developed to support the integration of disadvantaged young people into societies by both developing their skills and through ways of managing and addressing social inequality in society at large. There is a *living in community* dimension to social pedagogy often referred to as 'sharing the lifespace' – in which everyday events and routines of living are invoked to promote growth, development and learning. Valuing the lifespace is *valuing the 'seemingly mundane'* (Smith, 2011: 15) and is quite opposite to planned time-limited interventions. Promoting *democratic values* within shared spaces implies relatively flat hierarchies both within staff groups and between children or clients and adults. The expressive arts and outdoor education both have an important place in social pedagogy – they facilitate *doing and being together*, around which relationships of authenticity and meaning can flourish.

Social pedagogy has lived with the tension between being, on the one hand, an educational, integrationist and normative project and, on the other, 'a thorn in the flesh' of officialdom, where social pedagogues seek to transform societies on behalf of the freedom and justice of their (usually disadvantaged) clients (Lorenz, 1994). This tension arguably plays out in the UK today, where governmental support for social pedagogy through policies and policy measures are sought and prized, and standards and qualifications are established. However, the mission of social pedagogy is not to keep things as they are, but to point out and address injustice, and support people to equip themselves to address injustices. In this sense, social pedagogy *is a political project*.

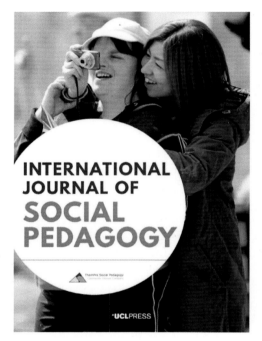

This is the cover for the *International Journal of Social Pedagogy*, established by Pat Petrie and Gabriel Eichsteller in 2009. The cover photo was selected from nominations from the growing social pedagogy community, who were asked to submit their expressions of social pedagogy. It captures the close relationship between adult and child, shared learning, the joy of discovering something together – often referred to as a 'common third' activity.

The relationship between education and social pedagogy can be close or distant, depending on whether education is defined in a broad or narrow sense. The scope for social pedagogy in the UK has mostly been applied to the domains of practice associated with children's social care, although it has overlaps and resonances with related human professions such as work with people with learning disabilities, supported housing, work with older people, youth work, alternative schooling and early childhood education.

What research findings support education in its broadest sense?

I am now going to turn to the findings of three major cross-national studies undertaken since 2000 in order to argue that education in its broadest sense (aka social pedagogy) is a valuable framework for responding to children in today's care and education services. The studies are:

- Care Work in Europe: Current understandings and future directions
- Residential Care in Denmark, Germany and England
- YiPPEE: Education of children in care.

Care Work in Europe: Current understandings and future directions

This was a six-nation mixed-method study examining *the quality of employment in care work* across settings addressing different target age groups (Cameron and Moss, 2007). We defined 'care work' as an umbrella term to refer to many kinds of services that attend to human need, but which focus on:

1. early childhood education and care services
2. day care, home-based care and residential care for older people
3. day care, home-based care and residential care for people with disabilities.

The participant countries were Denmark, Sweden, Hungary, Spain, the Netherlands and the UK (in practice, England). We considered the quality of employment not just in terms of the conditions of work, but also in the sense of what practitioners did, what skills and knowledge they relied on, and how they were developing as practitioners. We found the highest-quality employment to be in Denmark and Sweden, and this coincided with the most developed understandings of the social pedagogue (or its variant).

Beyond these variations in employment quality, we found many similarities between the different forms of care work in terms of what practitioners were actually doing. They were forming relationships, being attentive and responding to need, making finely tuned decisions about what should happen next to enhance quality of life or development or group dynamics. But the connections between the various forms of care work were rarely made in training or policy. The Danish pedagogue was a rare exception, as the training was for working with people aged 0–100 and the main occupation was pitched at bachelor degree level.

We included an innovative visual cue methodology to investigate cross-cultural variations in interpreting the same phenomena in different cultural contexts. We made six films in three countries, one each in early childhood education and care (ECEC) and older people's residential care. We then asked groups of practitioners and other knowledgeable experts to comment on the films, bringing in their own reflections on their expertise in the process (Cameron, 2007).

Film extract of Danish children.

Photo: Care Work in Europe

The Danish analysis showed that not only was play and learning valued in early childhood settings, it was also respected in everyday life. They referred to:

> togetherness and necessary activities in day-to-day life, such as eating, sleeping, going to the bathroom, going for a walk, saying hello and goodbye to parents...

> Some are routines and are repeated every day ... Such everyday life actions are a core value [in Danish early childhood settings]. Much time and space is given over to them. They are important ... for the

child becoming resourceful, independent and capable of living in society. (Jensen, 2011: 147)

There is a clear foundation here for education for life, developing skills for collaborative and democratic civic engagement between children and between children and adults. It is a multidimensional education, in which physical, cognitive and social education and care are all integrated. Blowing a child's nose, for example, is seen as an important part of pedagogical work as it offers an opportunity for an educational encounter, and for taking responsibility for the whole person. This holistic recognition of children leads, in Denmark, to fairly flat staff hierarchies in care institutions, as *the manner in which* routine tasks are carried out is valued as part of the pedagogical role. The pedagogue's role is also important for her or his ability to bring joy and lightness to the atmosphere of the early childhood setting, and to help children experience a wide range of emotions, perhaps especially when working outdoors. Taking physical risks, whether as a toddler climbing in and out of a sandbox, or helping to tend a campfire, are seen as learning opportunities.

Study participants who were practitioners in the UK were rather envious of the Danish kindergartens they could see on the videos. They were acutely aware of how hemmed in they were in comparison, with restricted outdoor space and external regulations that focused on averting risk rather than critically evaluating the benefits of everyday life activities in nurseries.

The cross-national work highlighted clear differences between practitioners working with and looking after young children in differing cultural contexts. These cultural differences extend to the concepts we use to describe and assess the work. Take the concept of 'competence' in education and care work. This has become a constrained idea in the English-language debate. It is about working to prescribed standards and evaluating practice in terms of being 'good enough'. The employment of a tick-box approach to measuring attainment of goals promotes measurement of those things that are easy to see. It risks neglecting a more nuanced approach, where the exercise of situated judgement, so strongly associated with quality of employment, has a diminished role in everyday practice (Cameron and Moss, 2007; Cameron, 2008).

I have focused on the Danish *paedagog* in early childhood settings, whose basic education is already at a high level, and for whom there is ample opportunity for subsequent continuous professional development. In England, by contrast, there is a medley of qualifications for early childhood education and care practice, which, despite considerable policy attention in the past 20 years, is still divided between teacher education for school settings for children aged 2–3 and up, and care-oriented occupations for working with children in non-school settings and for younger age groups.

Early childhood workforce

The *Care Work in Europe* study concluded that the quality of employment was significantly linked to the quality of the care work, and the value ascribed to it. Where it was defined as 'care' work, it tended to attract a low-skilled workforce; little education was required on entry and it offered low pay and societal recognition. Where it was defined as social pedagogy, or education, it attracted higher value. At the time of this research, in the early 2000s, there was considerable policy interest in improving outcomes for children through investing in the workforce. Ed Balls, as Minister for Children, declared that:

> a world class workforce (was the) single most important factor in achieving our ambitions for children and young people. Excellent practice by committed and passionate workers changes young lives. (DCSF, Foreword, 2020 Children and Young People's Workforce Strategy)

In the *Every Child Matters* and *Care Matters* (HM Treasury, 2003; DfES, 2006) policy papers, the occupation of social pedagogue was suggested as an option for both early childhood education and for residential care. In relation to early childhood, this idea was dropped in favour of the early years professional, then the early years teacher/educator. While the principle of joining up care and education for young children was accepted, the occupational models adopted did not take on board the depth (degree-level study for at least half of those working with children under compulsory school age) or the breadth of the Danish social pedagogue approach. Critical components of the quality of employment, notably pay and conditions, were not, and still have not been, addressed (Hevey, 2017).

Residential Care in Denmark, Germany and England

The mention of social pedagogue in policy was as a result of our studies of *Residential Care in Denmark, Germany and England.*

Working with Children in Care: European Perspectives (Petrie *et al.*, 2006) reported findings from studies focusing on the policy and professional educational environment, the practice operation and the experiences of young people and staff in residential care in Denmark, Germany, Flanders, France, the Netherlands and England. In the countries outside England, a broadly social pedagogic framework was in place, where education and upbringing framed the goals of state care for children and young people. Group life was valued, frequently characterized by *doing things*, often of a creative and practical nature, together, and of *being together*, or inhabiting the same life space.

Drawing of a 'good' social pedagogue illustrating the role of action and reflection.

credit: Danish study participant (Petrie *et al.*, 2006)

From interviews with 144 staff and 56 heads of establishment, and 302 young people, and by examining the records in 49 residential centres in Denmark, Germany and England, we found that the characteristics of the workforce were highly related to outcomes for young people.

In Denmark and Germany, those working in residential care were more likely to have higher-level qualifications, more likely to regard working with children's problems, team work with colleagues and their leaders as positive aspects of their work than in those working in England. In terms of relational practice, there were again cross-national differences. Residential care workers in the English sites were more likely to define their approach to providing emotional support as discursive (offering strategies, persuading), followed by an empathic approach (listening, naming feelings, offering a hug, spending time together), while in the other two countries this sequence was reversed and they were more likely to offer empathy and then a discursive approach.

Outlooks on keyworking responsibilities also differed. In England, there was a focus on procedures and short-term behaviour management, while under a social pedagogic framework there was a relational and longer-term development orientation. For young people, rates of participation in education and employment were higher in the Continental European countries, suggesting they enjoyed better social integration, and were associated with raised expectations of young people, such as prevalence of policies about continuing in education. There were pronounced country differences in the rate of teenage pregnancies among young people in the residential homes visited for the study, with the rate in England being three times that of Denmark and twice that in Germany. These differences were largely explained by staff characteristics associated with in-service training, practice responses and intention to continue in post – the working environment. Wide differences in the rate of criminal offences of residents (1.73 per resident in England, 0.092 in Germany and 0.158 in Denmark) were again found not to relate to the young people's characteristics but to the working environment (staff-child ratio) and practice responses (calling in external sources of support). Higher staff-child ratios were associated with poorer child outcomes.

These findings, and more, provided compelling evidence that the profession of social pedagogue, the working environment and a social pedagogic policy framework were all contributing to a coherent and more positive quality of life for young people in residential care than was happening in England. In particular, the Danish model of social pedagogue, with a foundation in higher-level educational qualifications for those working with children, young people, families and individuals, across a range of settings, coupled with investment in the group setting as a good-quality place of employment, shone as a highly developed practice example from which to learn.

Clearly it would be difficult to transfer the Danish model to England. But the Labour government did commission a pilot to investigate the effectiveness of social pedagogy in residential care, and this was carried out by employing social pedagogues trained in Germany and elsewhere to work in residential care provision in England (Cameron *et al.*, 2011). This work, and other pilots and capacity-building, led to the development of the Social Pedagogy Professional Association (SPPA) in the UK.

YiPPEE: Education of children in care

Entirely neglected for decades, the education of children in care is now mandated in policy and (usually) expected in practice. This is a dramatic turnaround and due in no small part to the probing work of Sonia Jackson over decades. In 2007, Sonia and I began a five-nation study called YiPPEE, which examined the educational pathways of care leavers (Jackson and Cameron, 2012). This was another mixed-method study that included surveys of local authorities, interviews with key policy actors and professionals, biographical narrative interviews with young people who had been in care, and analysis of national statistics.

	Denmark	England	Hungary	Spain	Sweden	TOTAL
Managers/professionals	5	9	4	13	8	**39**
Telephone screening interviews	75	74	133	132	53	**467**
Young people intensive sample first round	35	32	35	35	33	**170**
Young people second round	29	27	33	28	26	**143**
Nominated adults	14	18	34	20	25	**111**
TOTAL	**158**	**160**	**239**	**228**	**145**	**930**

YiPPEE: Interviews conducted in each country

In all of the countries studied (Denmark, England, Hungary, Spain, Sweden), young people who had been in care as children and who had some educational qualifications at age 16 were far less likely to go on to higher education than their contemporaries who had not been in care. Typically, by age 16, they have already fallen seriously behind, with fewer than half achieving the expected level at that stage at the same time as their birth cohort. At the upper secondary phase, fewer young people from care backgrounds compared to others held sufficient qualifications to continue in education, and this was particularly the case in England (14 versus 66 per cent). In all countries, many young people from care backgrounds dropped out of upper secondary education. Guidance on educational options tended to be of low quality and confusing. If young people were living independently, they tended to have multiple demands on their lives, including managing their own tenancies and household bills, frequent crises in their personal lives, and friendships and kin relations to maintain. Many of the young people interviewed had also experienced family bereavement during childhood. Their family backgrounds were characterized by serious maltreatment, chaotic domestic lives and little or no modelling of participation in further or higher education. However, of the 32 participants interviewed in-depth in England, 25 were in higher education and many were also working, had done or were doing voluntary work or participated in leisure activities.

Looking at what was happening in other countries shone an important light on practice. The incidence of care placement disruption was higher in England than in the other countries, so the children's childhoods tended to be less stable. But in some cases (Spain and Hungary), stability went hand in hand with low expectations from the adults around them, which could condemn able young people to a cycle of low-skilled, low-paid jobs. Economic survival was the most important criterion and there was no help from the state once they left the care service in these countries. This was in sharp contrast to young people who were not from a care background, whose parents would typically extend support for many years and in a variety of ways. In the Scandinavian countries, continuing educational opportunities and support for independent lives as young adults largely built on stable and loving foster care as children, or constructive, learning-oriented residential care. Several Danish young people had taken up an opportunity to spend a year in a boarding school when aged 15. The care leavers we spoke to had found this experience to be very helpful in forging relationships with adults, who were social pedagogues, and teachers, who were able to guide them to thinking about their future as integrated into society, and inspire them to study further.

The YiPPEE study underscored the hugely important role of *educators* (social pedagogues and those charged with the day-to-day care of young people in helping shape their educational fortunes, such as foster carers). The role of educators ranged from ensuring children in care attended school – indeed had a school to go to – to supporting their out-of-school interests and talents and motivating them to pursue their academic and practical ambitions in higher education settings. Without such support, young people are not likely to be 'enabled to reach educational levels substantially higher than their parents […], leading to stable and rewarding employment, [and] they are at great risk of slipping back as adults into the extremely disadvantaged social stratum from which they originated, undoing any beneficial effects of their care experience' (Jackson and Cameron, 2012: 1113).

Taken together, these three studies demonstrated the breadth of educational response required for children, particularly those in care and care leavers. Learning from social pedagogic and broad education approaches means supporting children's well-being through meaningful relationships. It also means providing children and young people with accurate guidance and practical help to navigate complex worlds as critical parts of our 'response' to them. Supporting well-being is a complex endeavour that goes beyond 'care' – indeed, it suggests reframing care as broadly *educative*, and reframing carers as 'educators' who are experts in everyday life (Cameron *et al.*, 2015). In addition, there should be recognition of young people's active contribution to their interior and their social lives, in terms of their self-esteem and civic engagement (Smith *et al.*, 2017), and societal structures including legal systems should be able to respond to children in a broadly *educational* frame.

I now turn to the last of my themes, which is the ongoing work investigating the scope, meaning and impact of practitioner-young person relationships.

Belonging

A return to the importance of relationships as a medium for practice with looked-after children was signalled by the House of Commons Education Select Committee report on children in care in 2009 when it stated:

> the failure of the care system to replicate or compensate for the stable relationships that most children have with their parents is one of its most serious and long-standing deficiencies. Even when all the right frameworks and structures are in place, it is the *quality of relationships* that will determine whether a child in care feels *cared about* on a day-to-day basis. (House of Commons Children, Schools and Families Committee, 2009: 27, emphasis added)

What is meant by 'quality of relationships'? In the UK, there has been a long-standing if sometimes implicit reliance on attachment theory to define professional-child relationships. Attachment theory foregrounds secure mother-infant relationships as essential for human development. Policy for looked-after children has often envisaged a (re-)instatement or replication of that one-to-one, mother-centric idea as important, hence foster care (largely by women) in domestic settings. It is instructive that the focus of the House of Commons statement was on being 'cared about'. In Continental Europe it might have been phrased as 'a good upbringing' or 'educated'.

My enquiry into relational practice in social pedagogic frameworks (Cameron, 2013) found more diversity in terms of the purpose of professional-child relationships. Professionals working with looked-after children in Belgium, Germany and Denmark, where group settings such as residential care are more common than in England, found four main purposes:

- sharing everyday lifespace/building skills
- an encounter without ulterior purpose/being together in the here and now
- a vehicle for emancipation/creating good conditions for young people to take action
- gaining an understanding of problems in order to 'get a change from before' and 'he tells me so I understand' (study participants).

A main underpinning for relationships is trust, which, according to the study participants, should be built on mutuality, reliability and continuity, as well as taking concrete action to create and support young people's opportunities in life. Attachment theory was considered to have a minimal role in the responses to questions about how relationships were formed and what their purpose was.

Critique of attachment

By contrast, in the UK, attachment theory has become even more dominant. A search for 'foster care' and 'theory' on Google shows up attachment-related programmes and little else. Schools have become a focus for attachment work. In 2015, NICE released guidelines on children's attachment, which stated:

> Schools and other education providers should ensure that all staff who may come into contact with children and young people with

attachment difficulties receive appropriate training on attachment difficulties. (para. 1.2.1)

But despite policies, programmes and practices around attachment, children's upbringing and belonging in care have not been secured. Placement disruption is still common, including among foster care placements intended to be long term (Biehal *et al.*, 2010). The rate of adoption is dropping while the rate of admission to care is going up (DfE, 2017). Much of the increase is among older groups of young people, where, arguably, the concept of attachment is even less relevant. In my paper with Smith and Reimer (2017), we argued that warm, affectionate relationships are undoubtedly needed, but that attachment theory has occupied too much theoretical space in social work and related debates about out-of-home care. We turn, instead, to longer-term and holistic recognition of children and young people – following Axel Honneth's three-dimensional recognition theory. The dimensions are love, solidarity and self-esteem. These dimensions recognize the inter-personal and the intimate, and the social and legal relationships of our lives, and argue that human growth and development require attention to all of them. This shares common ground with the social pedagogues' perspectives on relationships as being embedded in the environment as well as from person to person.

A multidimensional concept of belonging

A multidimensional concept of *belonging* offers a way forward when thinking about the impact of relationships with and responding to children and young people.

In theorizing about children living away from their parents, a 'sense of belonging' has been associated with long-term care and permanence. Belonging signifies a stable, committed foster placement (for no one belongs in so-called 'last resort' residential care), and an absence of divided loyalties. Here, children are wanted and feel part of a family and there is an expectation that this will continue over time (Biehal *et al.*, 2010; Boddy, 2013). This debate is highly influenced by attachment theory. Arguably, it fails to take account of the complexity of young people's lives in care. Fresh questions are needed about what it means to belong and whether and to what extent this is felt by young people in care.

A reworked concept of belonging might begin with the following definition: belonging is about 'being *at ease with oneself* and one's surroundings' (Miller, 2003). Belonging is:

> the quintessential mode of being human … in which all aspects of the self, as human, are perfectly integrated. (Miller, 2003: 218)

Also:

> Belonging involves a process of *creating a sense of identification* with one's social, relational and material surroundings. (May, 2011: 368)

It is also:

> a mode of being in which *we are as we ought to be*: fully ourselves. (Miller, 2003: 218)

So, to belong involves active work on the self and the surroundings – and the surroundings are to be considered multidimensional. Further, to belong is not a static concept but one that evolves over time and is perceived differently in different contexts; one can belong to multiple groups, social contexts – and families. Vanessa May (2011: 370) writes: 'few of us feel a sense of belonging merely to one group, culture or place but rather experience multiple senses of belonging' and says it is not 'something that we accomplish once and for all. Because the world and the people in it, including ourselves, are constantly undergoing change, belonging is something we have to keep achieving through an active process.' There are also structural impositions and obstructions to belonging, such as immigration rules, and expressions of prejudice are effective ways of stating who does not belong (Yuval-Davies, 2011). Bringing various perspectives on belonging together, we might say there are three main dimensions:

- social/relational – the immediate here and now
- cultural/historical – familiarity through what one brings from the past and ways of being
- embodied/geographical – touch, surroundings, place.

So, in thinking about how we might respond in terms of educationally oriented places for bringing up looked-after children, we might begin with broadening the indicators for belonging. For example, in my study of the meanings of 'home' within residential care (with Alison Clark and Stefan Kleipoedszus), we drew attention to the importance of objects, and familiarity with the situating of objects, when moving from place to place (Clark *et al.*, 2013). Selecting objects to decorate the mantelpiece and the kitchen is a good example of practices that support (or not) the third dimension of embodied or geographical belonging.

The sideboard: 'Having plants in the house is what you would have at your own home. We always have fruits and vegetables available for the young people.' (Pat, staff)

Photo: Clark *et al.*, 2013

In this conceptualization, belonging is created, not through the 'sense' of an individual, but by being nurtured in the present, through daily interactions, in having shared memories and reference points, and objects of familiarity from the past, and in the ways in which the physical and legal landscape puts one at ease. This is not to say that every child must be perfectly matched with a placement and cannot tolerate difference, but that far more attention needs to be paid, within the support system for children and for foster carers and residential care, to meeting the young person, and their environment, at any one moment.

Recent work as part of a Swiss-German-English study on the processes of foster care breakdown, which examined how these dimensions of belonging mapped onto the experience of foster care, showed that while foster carers in England were familiar with the social/relational, and worked hard on this, there was far less evidence of the other two dimensions of belonging (cultural/historical and embodied/geographical) (Cameron and Hauari, 2018).

In the cases we examined, placements began as an emergency, seemed to go well initially and then became longer term with little active planning. But the foster carers had little information about the young people beforehand and, being thrust into a new situation straight away, were rarely able to comprehend and meet cultural/historical familiarity. There was little focus in the preparation for placements on the physical landscape, objects, the place of care and accepting physical touch.

If belonging is fundamentally about being at ease with oneself, arguably it is relevant for all out-of-home placements, not just those in long-term foster care, and from the moment a placement begins. Multidimensional belonging practices require all those involved in out-of-home placements to reflect on the concrete everyday life consequences of a new life space.

How should we respond to children in care today?

A focus on belonging helps us to envision the upbringing, developmental and educational 'project' of responding in practice and policy to children in out-of-home care. We are currently living through an era of much insecurity and fracturing of the civic, political and social body. Inequalities are rising and support services that ameliorate the impact of inequalities are diminishing. Young people in out-of-home placements are in danger of being at the centre of a perfect storm of impoverished resources, poor recognition of staff and underdeveloped knowledge bases for professional practice, so that young people come to official attention as criminal or mentally ill, and the potential to make a constructive and long-lasting difference to their everyday lives is rarely visible.

The 'red thread' through the research I have talked about today argues for:

- everyday life with practical, relational and curiosity-driven meaning as well as potential outcomes for children and young people in care
- 'care' seen as education and upbringing – a developmental as well as a nurturing and caretaking task
- educators who adopt a reflective, critical position, a humanistic stance as well as relational empathy
- educators who forge, nurture and, together, enjoy creative and practical opportunities for young people as well as taking them to school and helping with homework.

This is essentially a social pedagogic stance on how we respond to children and young people. It is to argue that neither 'good' attachment relationships nor outcome-oriented performance-driven 'education' are enough on their own to address flourishing through belonging for children in care. A rounded approach is needed, so that every encounter is an educational opportunity, on which educators can reflect and evaluate in its context. Neither is it enough to push all the 'response' onto the educator: systems and processes within welfare states support (or not) young people's belonging and flourishing too. This means a political response is necessary; support services, such as children's centres and nursery schools, which nurture education (knowledge) and belonging (being at ease), are required not just for children at risk of being in care but for all children and families. The consequences of austerity-driven withdrawal of financial support to children's services will surely show up in rises in admissions to children's social care services, making our response more critical than ever.

References

Biehal, N., Ellison, S., Baker, C. and Sinclair, I. (2010) *Belonging and Permanence: Long-term outcomes in foster care and adoption*. London: British Association for Adoption and Fostering.

Boddy, J. (2013) 'Understanding permanence for looked after children: A review of research for the Care Inquiry'. Online. http://sro.sussex.ac.uk/44711/1/Boddy_2013_Understanding_Permanence.pdf (accessed 15 January 2018).

Boddy, J., Cameron, C., Moss, P., Mooney, A., Petrie, P. and Statham, J. (2005) *Introducing Pedagogy into the Children's Workforce: Children's Workforce Strategy: A response to the consultation document*. London: Thomas Coram Research Unit.

Butler, P. (2017) 'Austerity policy blamed for record numbers of children taken into care'. *The Guardian*, 11 October. Online. www.theguardian.com/society/2017/oct/11/austerity-policy-blamed-record-numbers-children-taken-into-care (accessed 7 January 2018).

Cameron, C. (1990) 'Kilquhanity's Jubilee: Reflections and creations, 1940–1990'. Online. www.braehead.info/html/kilquhanity_jubilee.html (accessed 3 January 2018).

Cameron, C. (2007) 'Understandings of care work with young children: Reflections on children's independence in a video observation study'. *Childhood*, 14 (4), 467–86.

Cameron, C. (2008) 'What do we mean by "competence"?'. *Children in Europe*, 15, 12–13.

Cameron, C. (2013) 'Cross-national understandings of the purpose of professional–child relationships: Towards a social pedagogical approach'. *International Journal of Social Pedagogy*, 2 (1), 3–16.

Cameron, C. (2016) *Leaving Care and Employment in Five European Countries: An undocumented problem?* Innsbruck: SOS Children's Villages International.

Cameron, C., Connelly, G. and Jackson, S. (2015) *Educating Children and Young People in Care: Learning placements and caring schools.* London: Jessica Kingsley Publishers.

Cameron, C. and Hauari, H. (2018) 'Supporting foster carers and young people during "breakdown": The contribution of "belonging"'. Presentation to Abbrüche von Pflegeverhältnissen im Kinder- und Jugendalter, Zurich, 22 January 2018.

Cameron, C., Hauari, H. and Hollingworth, K. (forthcoming) *Leaving Care, Employability and "Decent Work" in 11 Countries Worldwide: Final report for SOS Children's Villages International.* Vienna: SOS Children's Villages International.

Cameron, C., Hollingworth, K., Schoon, I., van Santen, E., Schröer, W., Ristikari, T., Heino, T. and Pekkarinen, E. (submitted) *Care Leavers in Early Adulthood: How do they fare in England, Finland and Germany?* Child and Youth Services Review.

Cameron, C. and Moss, P. (2007) *Care Work in Europe: Current understandings and future directions.* London: Routledge.

Cameron, C., Petrie, P., Wigfall, V., Kleipoedszus, S. and Jasper, A. (2011) *Final Report of the Social Pedagogy Pilot Programme: Development and implementation.* London: Thomas Coram Research Unit.

Carroll, C. and Cameron, C. (2017) *Taking Action for Looked After Children in School: A knowledge exchange programme.* London: UCL Institute of Education Press.

CBI/Pearson (2016) *The Right Combination: CBI/Pearson Education and Skills Survey 2016.* London: CBI/Pearson. Online. www.cbi.org.uk/cbi-prod/assets/File/pdf/cbi-education-and-skills-survey2016.pdf (accessed 3 January 2018).

Clark, A., Cameron, C. and Kleipoedszus, S. (2013) 'Sense of place in children's residential care homes: Perceptions of home?'. *Scottish Journal of Residential Child Care*, 13 (2), 1–18.

DCSF (Department for Children, Schools and Families) (2008) '2020 Children and Young People's Workforce Strategy'. Nottingham DCSF Publications.

DfE (Department for Education) (2017) 'Children looked after in England (including adoption), year ending 31 March 2017 (SFR 50/2017)'. Statistical First Release, 28 September. Online. www.gov.uk/government/uploads/system/uploads/attachment_data/file/664995/SFR50_2017-Children_looked_after_in_England.pdf (accessed 3 January 2018).

DfES (Department for Education and Skills) (2006) 'Care matters: Transforming the lives of children and young people in care'. Cm 6932, London, The Stationery Office.

Eurydice (2009) *National Testing of Pupils in Europe: Objectives, organisation and use of results.* Brussels: Education, Audiovisual and Culture Executive Agency. Online. http://eacea.ec.europa.eu/education/eurydice/documents/thematic_reports/109EN.pdf (accessed 3 January 2018).

Fielding, M. (2005) 'Alex Bloom, pioneer of radical state education'. *FORUM*, 47 (2–3), 119–34.

Hastings, A., Bailey, N., Bramley, G., Gannon, M. and Watkins, D. (2015) *The Cost of the Cuts: The impact on local government and poorer communities.* York: Joseph Rowntree Foundation. Online. www.jrf.org.uk/sites/default/files/jrf/migrated/files/Summary-Final.pdf (accessed 3 January 2018).

Hevey, D. (2017) *United Kingdom of Great Britain and Northern Ireland ECEC Workforce Profile*. Munich: State Institute of Early Childhood Research. Online. www.seepro.eu/English/pdfs/UNITED_KINGDOM_ECEC%20Workforce.pdf (accessed 7 January 2018).

HM Treasury (2003) 'Every child matters'. Cm 5860, London, The Stationery Office.

House of Commons Children, Schools and Families Committee (2009) *Looked-after children: Third report of session 2008–09, Volume 1*. London, House of Commons. Online. https://publications.parliament.uk/pa/cm200809/cmselect/cmchilsch/111/111i.pdf (accessed 15 January 2018).

Jackson, S. and Cameron, C. (2012) 'Leaving care: Looking ahead and aiming higher'. *Children and Youth Services Review*, 34 (6), 1107–14.

Jensen, J.J. (2011) 'Understandings of Danish pedagogical practice'. In Cameron, C. and Moss. P. (eds) *Social Pedagogy and Working with Children and Young People: Where care and education meet*. London: Jessica Kingsley Publishers.

Joseph Rowntree Foundation (2017) 'UK poverty 2017: A comprehensive analysis of poverty trends and figures'. Report by the JRF Analysis Unit, York, JRF.

Lorenz, W. (1994) *Social Work in a Changing Europe*. London: Routledge.

May, V. (2011) 'Self, belonging and social change'. *Sociology*, 45 (3), 363–78.

Miller, L. (2003) 'Belonging to country: A philosophical anthropology'. *Journal of Australian Studies*, 27 (76), 215–23.

Moss, P. and Petrie, P. (2002) *From Children's Services to Children's Spaces: Public policy, children and childhood*. London: RoutledgeFalmer.

NICE (National Institute for Clinical Excellence) (2015) 'Children's attachment: Attachment in children and young people who are adopted from care, in care or at high risk of going into care'. Online. www.nice.org.uk/guidance/ng26 (accessed 15 January 2018).

Petrie, P., Boddy, J., Cameron, C., Wigfall, V. and Simon, A. (2006) *Working with Children in Care: European perspectives*. Maidenhead: Open University Press.

Schoon, I. and Lyons-Amos, M. (2017) 'A socio-ecological model of agency: The role of psycho-social and socioeconomic resources in shaping education and employment transitions in England'. *Longitudinal and Lifecourse Studies*, 8 (1), 35–56. Online. www.llcsjournal.org/index.php/llcs/article/view/404/486.

Smith, M. (2011) 'Working in the "lifespace"'. In *In Residence*. Glasgow: Scottish Institute for Residential Child Care, 12–19. Online. www.celcis.org/files/8614/3878/4830/In-residence-a_series-of-12-papers.pdf (accessed 7 January 2018).

Smith, M.K. (2015) 'What is education? A definition and discussion'. Online. http://infed.org/mobi/what-is-education-a-definition-and-discussion/ (accessed 7 January 2018).

Smith, M., Cameron, C. and Reimer, D. (2017) 'From attachment to recognition for children in care'. *British Journal of Social Work*, 47 (6), 1606–23.

Yuval-Davis, N. (2011) *The Politics of Belonging: Intersectional Contestations*. London: Sage.